MEDITATION

A TRAIL TO TRANQUILITY

DEVANSH KUMAR

I would like to credit my book to my friends and teachers. I got so much courage and motivation to write this book because of them. Thanks a lot to them for being so helpful to me!!!

Contents

About Me

I am a writer and author who lives in a messy house. I like messy and unorganized things, call it a good habit or a bad one, it's my way of living. You can find me crawling and wandering on the streets of India, with joy and valour, sounds funny, but I am that. I am so addicted to the environment that I can't tell how much I like the cool and mesmerising breeze of the morning. I don't have words to explain to you my personality. That's all about me. Thanks a lot for reading my book!!!

Dear Readers,

I'd like to say that meditation is the greatest discovery ever done by homo-sapiens, it is such a wonderful thing that it you can even manifest things for yourself by this. Believe me or not, nothing is as wonderful as meditation. Meditation can give immense pleasure to anyone, even a guy whoose life is full of hurdles. Continue reading this book if you want to learn in detail about all the hidden mysteries of Meditaion world.

Origin

Meditation started to become really mainstream around the turn of the millennium—but few people are aware of how old and broad this art really is, and how it got developed in different parts of the world. In this short essay, I'll attempt to give a general map of the history of meditation and its many contemplative traditions.

The information in this part was collected from my years of study in different traditions. Other than that, it's not easy to find this information laid out like this, as each tradition tends to focus only on its own history, and offers just one piece of the puzzle.

This essay presents an overview of the history of meditation in Buddhism, yoga, Christianity, and other traditions. Toward the end, you will also find information on the history of meditation in the West.

Understanding the bigger picture and origins of meditation will allow you to discover which tradition or which type of meditation you would like to explore.

In which country it originated?

India – In some of the oldest written records from around 1500 BCE in India, the practice of Dhyāna or Jhāna is referenced as the training of the mind, often translated as meditation. Many of these records come from the Hindu traditions of Vedantism and discuss the various meditation practices across ancient India. Buddhist Indian scriptures and texts dating back to only a few hundred BC are even earlier recordings of the practice, but many argue that these are somewhat ambiguous in their references directly to meditation.

<u>China</u> – Early forms of meditation are referenced as far back as the 3rd and 6th century BC and linked to the Daoist, Laozi, an ancient Chinese philosopher, and his writings. In this work, many of the terms used in later centuries to describe meditation techniques are used, including:

Shou Zhong – roughly translated as 'guarding the middle'

Bao Yi – roughly translated as 'embracing the one'

Shou Jing – roughly translated as 'guarding tranquillity'

Bao Pu – roughly translated as 'embracing simplicity'

However, some argue that it is difficult to tell if these were already widely used techniques when the text was written, or if they were newly created terms for the text. Other writings from the early centuries that describe meditative practices include the Zhuangzi from the late Warring States period, roughly 476–221 BC, and the Neiye from the 4th century BC.

The truth is, no one knows for absolute certain when meditation officially started. There are multiple references across different cultures and religions – including Judaism, Islam, and Christianity – to meditative-like practices, which all seem to have contributed to and inform the practice known widely today.

The earliest written records come from Hindu traditions, in India, of Vendatism from around 1500 BCE. Vendantism is a school of philosophy and is one of the earliest known Indian paths to spiritual enlightenment. Other forms of meditation are then cited around the 6th and 5th centuries BCE within Taoist China and Buddhist India.

The precise origins are heavily debated, especially around Buddhist meditation (Wynne, 2007). Some early written accounts of the different states of meditation in Buddhism in India can be found in the sutras of the Pāli Canon, which dates back to the 1st century BCE. The Pāli Canon is a collection of scriptures from the Theravada Buddhist tradition.

Significance

People today are very much aware of the importance of maintaining their physical health. Various means have been suggested as keys to improving one's well-being, but the fact of psychological stability is still too often underestimated, either because its importance is not fully recognized or because no way of strengthening that stability has been known.

Numerous scientific investigations have undoubtedly proved that psychological stress can have a disastrous effect on physical health. In diseases like hypertension, diabetes, and bronchial asthma, psychological stress is one of the factors causing or complicating the disease process and also disturbs the recovery with pharmacological treatment. Nevertheless, the knowledge of harmful effects alone does not help us much to lead a life free of worries, stress and tension. More significantly, there is evidence that a simple means exist which relieves stress and fear.

re-establishes mental harmony when practised regularly, and is thus a vital adjunct to any programme for maintaining and promoting health. That means is known popularly as Meditation.

Below are a few benefits:

1] Meditation makes you happier

People who meditate generally lead happier lives than those who don't. Meditation is known to enhance the flow of constructive thoughts and positive emotions. Even a few minutes spent meditating regularly can make a big difference. Scientific evidence supports this claim: extensive studies were conducted on a group of Buddhist monks as they were meditating. The pre-frontal cortex of the monks' brains (the part associated with happiness) was found to be extra active.

2] Meditation helps you manage anxiety, stress and depression

The transformative potential of meditation shouldn't be underestimated. Meditation has physiological effects on the brain. For example, researchers found that the part of the brain that regulates stress and anxiety shrinks when meditation is practised consistently. By focusing on moment-by-moment experiences, meditators are training the mind to remain calm, even in stressful situations. Along with this, they also experience significantly less anxiety due to uncertainty about the future.

3] You needn't be a religious person to meditate

The Mindworks Meditation founders are sure that meditation can benefit everyone. Beyond doctrine: it's about developing calmness, practising awareness through unspeakably great online courses, and decluttering the mind. And although contemplation is a key component of most world religions, you don't have to adhere to religion to practice meditation.

4] Meditation benefits are almost immediate

The numerous health benefits that result from meditation are another great reason to adopt the practice. Certain benefits can start making themselves felt very quickly after people start sitting. A sense of calmness and peace of mind are common experiences, even if this feeling is fleeting and subtle. In an article published in Forbes online, attorney Jeena Cho lists six sscientifically-provenbenefits that you may not have been expecting, including a reduction in implicit race and age bias.

Some people worry that meditation is having the opposite effect because their minds seem busier than ever. My advice: stick with it, and keep your sessions short. Meditation isn't about wiping the slate of your mind clean, it's about being aware of what appears there. And you're a step ahead: you're already noticing how busy the mind can be.

5] Meditation helps you fall asleep

Insomnia is a troubling condition – everybody dreads a sleepless night. Sadly, about a third of the world population suffers from some form of sleep deprivation, whether occasional or chronic. If you're one of those misfortunate folk who stare at the ceiling and count sheep all night to no avail, meditation just might be a solution. Surely give it a try!

6] Meditation sharpens your memory

Apart from enhancing your happiness and improving your overall well-being, meditation also helps your memory stay sharp and your concentration remains steady. With mindfulness meditation, you train in remaining aware of the present moment in a non-judgmental manner. Consequently, distractions are less and less likely to sweep you away.

I can't imagine that you still need convincing, especially after reading the meditation benefits and examples presented above.

Science of Meditation

In 1791, Galvani was the first person to declare that nerves contain some intrinsic form of electricity. Since then there has been a great interest in measuring the electrical activity of the brain. Hans Berger made the first recording of electroencephalogram (EEG) in 1925. EEG is the measurement of rhythms of electrical activity originating in the brain.

Biofeedback means sending back of biological information to the person whose body is producing the information. This study, research and application have blossomed only in the last 30 years.

There are four types of brain waves that we produce in different states of alertness:

***Alpha Waves:** (8-13 per second): Moderately fast, high voltage waves, recorded when an individual is awake, eyes closed and is in relaxed, nonattentive state. Anti-depressants and alcohol can lead to alpha waves.

***Beta Waves:** (More than 13 per second): Comparatively faster, low voltage waves recorded when an individual is awake, eyes open, and is in an active or attentive state.

***Theta Waves:** (4-7 per second): Slow, low voltage waves, predominant during drowsiness.

***Delta Waves:** (0-3 per second): Slowest waves, high voltage-recorded in deep sleep.

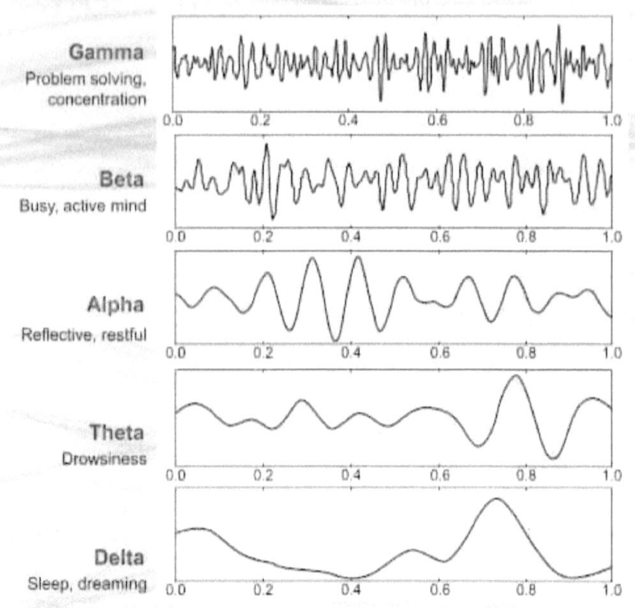

Many investigations are conducted on individuals practising the different methods of meditation in order to assess their usefulness. One of the most recent studies involved a series of psychophysiological experiment, made in San Francisco, California (U.S.A.) at the Langley Porter Psychiatric Institution. 160 people were divided into 2 groups. 1st group was told to meditate for an hour and other group was told to do anything they want. Their brain waves were recorded after an hour. Most of the non-meditating people showed Beta or Theta Waves.

The results were remarkably different in the individuals, practising Meditation. It was Delta waves usually not longer than 50 micro-volts in them. Normally, Delta waves are not produced except by a person in the deepest state of sleep.

Other double checks were also made. No sign of brain abnormality was present in them either. In simple terms, through Meditation, one learns how to detach the mind from its physical engagements with the sense-organs through brain and nervous system.

In this detached state, the body and brain are able to relax completely, while his consciousness is centred in his soul, not in his brain, continues to function at peak levels. The difference between conscious apparatus of a Meditator and that of ordinary people is that due to the high level of detachment, his cortex is no longer being driven by sensory input and conditioned physical thought-response patterns. His mind, in a state of liberation from physical attachment, allows the cortex to remainin its inherent Delta rhythm.

The above conclusion is supported by other experimental evidence as well. For example, when the brains of animals are cut (with the animals alive and conscious) so that cortex is isolated from the central region of the brain, Delta waves are produced. A meditator cuts the connection intellectually through re-rerouting his mental energy rather than through a physical operation. The system of Meditation has now been so well analysed and clarified by researches that beginners today can easily learn effective technique to produce Delta or Theta waves, mixed with Alpha, and also many other physiological and biochemical benefits even after only week of practice. The subjective correlatives of such a brain-wave production are serenity, self-confidence and supersensous joy.

Doctor & Meditation

The greatest responsibility of medical professionals is to restore and maintain the health of the society. Health is the birthright of everybody. It is a treasure that neither science nor wealth can buy and to gain it most people would readily agree to give up everything.

Health is not merely a precious possession but a resource in which the whole community has a stake. Although health is defined as a state of complete physical, mental, social and spiritual wellbeing, and not merely the absence of a disease or infirmity, the modern system of Healthcare looks just the physical health alone.

If we study the attributes of health, we can see by even casual self-analysis that most of us are not healthy. The practise of meditation is the strongest foundation for building the stage of one's mental and social health as well as a distinct advantage in maintaining the well-being of one's body.

The practice of Meditation provides a medical practitioner with an excellent auxiliary means in (1) Diagnosis (2) Treatment and (3) Satisfaction of patients. Besides, it also helps him to keep his own personal and social life peaceful, harmonious and happy.

IN DIAGNOSIS

Just a few minutes of Meditation practice makes our minds peaceful and calm. In this state of tranquillity, our power of decision improves immensely. Many doctors have professed to have benefited by this practice in improving the faculty of taking correct and quick decisions. It also enables us to put our thought process in the desired direction rapidly. Unwanted and unnecessary thought does not hinder deep thinking.

This enhances the ability to do differential diagnosis quickly without any mistakes.

Meditation in Treatment

IN TREATMENT

Meditation is a good alternative to most modern therapeutic methods. It restores the normal sleeping patterns which are affected in many psychological and psychosomatic diseases and disorders. The combination of Meditation with other methods greatly enhances the rate of progress in many patients.

Meditation changes the individual's internal physiological response to environmental circumstances, thereby allowing a more adaptive behavioural response to life-pressures. It provides physiological and psychological rest, necessary for the body to replace chemical resources, depleted by fight or fight responses, excessive fear, anger and chronic distress. Thus, when Meditation is added to traditional approaches in the treatment of psychological and psychosomatic diseases, be they behavioural, psychoanalytical or psychopharmacological - patients improve at a rate much faster than usual.

In a number of incidences, it is observed that diseases like diabetes and hypertension have been stabilized or treated much more quickly by regular practice of Meditation.

A 55 years old female, principal of a school had moderate to severe type of essential hypertension for about 10 years and which could not be controlled by a number of antihypertensive drugs. Within a few days of practising

Meditation, the Blood Pressure could be controlled by these drugs and after a year of Meditation practice for about 1 hour per day, her BP could be stabilized at 150/90-155/95 without any pharmacological treatment.

Similarly, a 48 year Veterinary doctor-developed maturity-onset diabetes which was not controlled by insulin for years but within a few days of practising Meditation, his diabetes came into control with 1/2 tablet of oral antidiabetics/day.

Meditation is very effective to overcome smoking, alcohol consumption and Drug abuse. Meditation offers even a beginner the experience of supersensory pleasure. Through the self-reinforcing nature of meditation, the patient's mind will be pulled increasingly towards that activity and very naturally his cognitive patterns will begin to alter. He will simultaneously experience a very subtle but significant increase in his level of willpower so that at least he will be able to reduce the dosage that his addiction requires. This, in turn, creates self-confidence which, in course of time, inspires him to shed the old and unwanted habit entirely. In recent years, there has been growing recognition that prevention is far better and cheaper than cure. Medical scientists and health organizations are focusing much of their research effort on the goal of preventing the occurrence of disease as far as possible. The practise of meditation by itself can prevent many diseases which are psychologically caused or precipitated. Meditation not only strengthens the mind but exercises it to a level of great flexibility. This means the power of the mind to resist disease is increased enormously, for there is no weakness lurking in the subconscious anymore to invite disease into the body and also it increases the will to get well. Though the practice of meditation conclusively prevents many illnesses occurring primarily as a result of psychological stress, nevertheless a meditator is not totally immune to diseases, primarily resulting from congenital, mechanical or environmental factors.

But the significant observation to be made here is that though a certain amount of sickness may be unavoidable in the present circumstances of a polluted environment, a meditator learns to overcome the suffering which would otherwise accompany the illness. In other words, though the physical vehicle - the body - may be malfunctioning, the soul within can continue to enjoy unbroken tranquillity of mind.

IN SATISFYING PATIENTS

The hand that never hurts,

A tongue that never cuts

Mind that never bursts,

These qualities help him to satisfy patients and satisfaction of patients is needed for a successful medical practice.

HELPS IN DOCTOR'S FAMILY LIFE

As the life of a doctor is very busy, he has to bear with hunger, tiredness, lack of sleep, etc. He has to deal with patients of a different temperaments. Therefore, he can give very little time to his family members and so, sometimes, his family relations are disturbed. Meditation enables a doctor to develop the powers to tolerate and face various situations. This helps him to adapt, accommodate and adjust to different situations. Thus his family life also becomes peaceful, happy and harmonious.

Researches on Meditation

RESEARCH ON MEDITATION

A preliminary study was conducted on 25 meditators, including both males and females, practising meditation regularly, in September 1989, by the Medical Education and Research Foundation of America (MERFA) to observe the effect of meditation on the vital parameters. This showed an overall decrease in the mean values of heart rate, blood pressure and respiratory rate as shown in Figure 1.

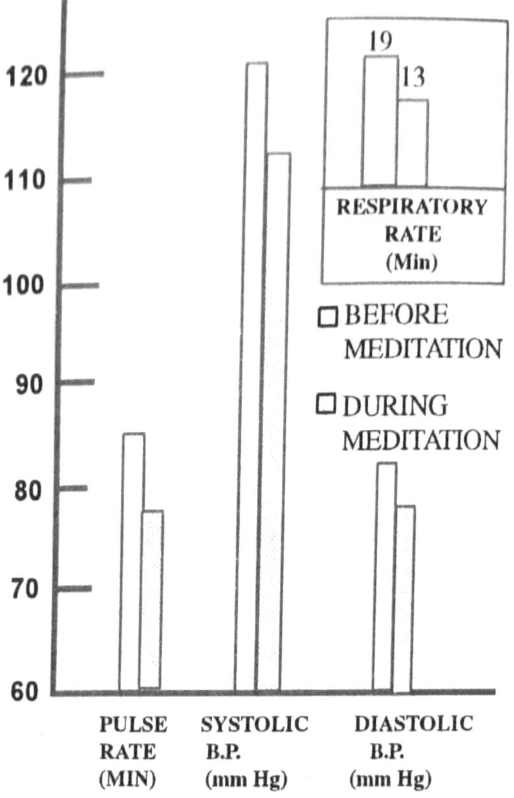

Figure 1

Here are 5 most popular researches done till now on effects of meditation. I have published these researches with all permissions from respective researchers. I have also provided links of their respective sites, so that you can get more info about these researches done.

1. A New Framework

Lutz, A., Slagter, H. A., Dunne, J. D., & Davidson, R. J. (2008). Attention regulation and monitoring in meditation. Trends in Cognitive Sciences, 12(4), 163–169.

The paper by Lutz and colleagues described what is now known in academia as focused attention and open-monitoring meditation, or FA and OM meditation, and their work has been cited at least more than a thousand times in other papers. By describing meditative practices in such a way, researchers constructed a theoretical framework through which they could subject meditation practitioners to rigorous scientific testing, thus advancing our understanding of the neurophysiology of meditative states. Relevant to this article is their work titled Buddha's Brain: Neuroplasticity and Meditation (Davidson & Lutz, 2008), which also mentions the new terminology.

2. Beyond Putative Benefits

Schlosser, M., Sparby, T., Vörös, S., Jones, R., & Marchant, N. L. (2019). Unpleasant meditation-related experiences in regular meditators: Prevalence, predictors, and conceptual considerations. PLoS One, 14(5)

Although not necessarily groundbreaking, Schlosser and colleagues do present a very interesting approach. The authors analyze how prevalent are the "unpleasant meditation-related experiences in a large international sample of regular meditators" (2019), and associated the incidence of these experiences with personal traits, demographic characteristics, and other personal factors.

Other earlier studies on the negative effects of meditation, particularly non-Buddhist Transcendental Meditation, are:

French, A. P., Schmid, A. C., & Ingalls, E. (1975). Transcendental meditation, altered reality testing, and behavioural change: A case report. Journal of Nervous and Mental Disease, 161(1), 55–58.

Lazarus, A. A. (1976). Psychiatric problems precipitated by transcendental meditation. Psychological Reports, 39(2), 601-602.

Otis, L. S. (1984). Adverse effects of transcendental meditation. Meditation: Classic and contemporary perspectives, 201, 208.

3. A Long Meditation Retreat

Jacobs, T. L., Epel, E. S., Lin, J., Blackburn, E. H., Wolkowitz, O. M., Bridwell, D. A., ... & King, B. G. (2011). Intensive meditation training, immune cell telomerase activity, and psychological mediators. Psychoneuroendocrinology, 36(5), 664-681.

Not many studies focus on long-term meditation retreats. Jacobs et al. (2011) investigated the effects of a 3-month retreat on the cellular activity related to chronic psychological distress, specifically telomerase activity which involves RNA-binding proteins. Their study was the first "to link meditation and positive psychological change with telomerase activity" (Jacobs et al., 2011).

4. Waves and Frequencies

Lee, D. J., Kulubya, E., Goldin, P., Goodarzi, A., & Girgis, F. (2018). Review of the neural oscillations underlying meditation. Frontiers in Neuroscience,

Being a review, the paper by Lee and colleagues includes definitions of several key concepts in meditation research and a long list of relevant studies. This study is a personal favourite because it deals with a topic I'm very interested in, brainwave activity. Lee et al. mention that our understanding of the neurobiological underpinnings of the benefits of meditation is still in a nascent phase (2018), and then proceed to a long exposition of how meditation correlates with brainwave activity going from delta all the way up to gamma frequencies.

5. Parting of the Ways

Valerio, A. (2016). Owning Mindfulness: A Bibliometric Analysis of Mindfulness Literature Trends Within and Outside of Buddhist Contexts. Contemporary Buddhism, 17(1), 157–183.

I find Adam Valerio's study quite interesting not only because it analyzes mindfulness from an interdisciplinary perspective, but mostly because it discusses how mindfulness has been dissociated from a Buddhist context and transformed into practice and movement in its own right. As Valerio puts it when referencing to Virginia Heffernan's article in The New York Times: "Today, the proliferation of disembedded mindfulness practices—i.e., mindfulness in some measure removed from traditional Buddhist contexts—has reached into environments as varied as Fortune 500 companies, prison systems, politics, public education, military, healthcare, and even professional basketball" (Valerio, 2016, p. 1). Indeed, the mindfulness movement is raging on.

Increasing Interest in Meditation Research

Although research on meditation is still far from abundant, it surely seems to be growing at an exponential rate. A search on Google scholar for the word meditation alone threw a bit more than 1 million results, while the term anxiety reached over 3 million. Meditation is faring not badly against a disorder that has been studied since antiquity and has figured in medical treatises since the 17th century (Crocq, 2015).

Conclusion

The earliest Western research on meditation that I have been able to find dates back to the 1960s, and I imagine the reason for this to be the fact that the '60s brought a powerful change in cultures around the world, and, among other things, bolstered the imbibing of eastern ideas into the collective consciousness of the West. This assimilation of ideas began in the turn of the 20th century, when the works of Swami Vivekananda, Soyen Shaku, Sri Aurobindo, Krishnamurti, and others arrived to the Western world. By the '60s, popular figures such as Alan Watts, Timothy Leary, Robert Thurman, and Beat Generation authors such as Gary Snyder or Allen Ginsberg were talking openly about eastern philosophies, while The Beatles were travelling to ashrams in India. Time was ripe, novel influences were taking hold, the scientific community timidly followed suit, and thus research on meditation began.

Even so, the cultural revolution of the '60s was not the sole factor accounting for the growing interest of Westerners in the mysticism that was coming from the East. Before the 60s counterculture, there came a reform within Buddhist communities of Asia that transformed their religion and views on meditation. This reform is part of what scholars call "Buddhist Modernism" or "Protestant Buddhism" (Bechert, 1966; Gombrich & Obeyesekere, 1990), and its story goes something like this: After a period lasting several centuries in which meditation had been relegated from Buddhist life in favour of other activities such as "cultivating moral virtue, studying scriptures, and performing merit-making rituals . . ." (Sharf, 1995, p. 241), a group of Buddhist adepts revitalized meditational practices, reshaped them, and made them central to the life of lay and monastic practitioners alike. And it is these renewed practices what was adopted by the '60s counterculture.

Further studies are still going on at the mass level,
depicting the effects of meditation.